AWAKEN THE GODS

Aphorisms to Remember The Way Home

Chuck Spezzano Ph.D.

A Psychology of Vision Book

Statements that have the power to change lives are called aphorisms. This is a collection of such sayings that impact to sudden clarity and make a difference in one's life.

Garnered from close to two decades of therapeutic insight, these sayings emerge from the mind of one who believes that life is not just about problems, but about vision; not just about repair, but about purpose.

WELLSPRING PUBLICATIONS LIMITED

46 Cyril Mansions, Prince of Wales Drive,
London SW11 4HW. England.

© 1991 Chuck Spezzano Ph.D.

ISBN. 0 9513520 7 5

Cover illustration: Vicki Bennett
Calligraphy: Margaret Davis

Printed in Great Britain by BPCC Wheatons Ltd, Exeter

ACKNOWLEDGEMENTS

I primarily acknowledge my wife for the love, support and true help that she has given me in making this aphorism book a reality. Her exceptional editorial ability and fine critical eye have added a lustre to this work that would otherwise have been missed.

Next, I would like to acknowledge Mark Wadleigh for his ideas about the title. Brian Mayne, of Wellspring Publications, was of great assistance to me in gathering many of the aphorisms. Also, I gratefully acknowledge many of my friends, and seminar participants who sent back aphorisms that I had spontaneously spoken in workshops.

In addition to my wife and my 19 years of work as a therapist, THE COURSE IN MIRACLES has been a constant source of inspiration and one from which I have garnered many of my ideas.

DEDICATION

I dedicate this book to my wife, Lencay, with deep appreciation for our journey together. Though I was the voice by which these aphorisms were spoken, we were the garden in which they grew.

When life has stopped unfolding
and has been reduced to dullness,
We crave a new birth,
A new beginning.
It is not something
that can be planned,
only asked for ·· and received.
Vision is not made; it is created.
It comes because we desire it wholly
And are willing
to be shown the answers.
The birth of Vision makes life new.

Failing
    is a form of power struggle
with a significant other
    from the past
    or the present.

All forms of miracles occur
through some form
of forgiveness.

Forgiveness
is a giving forth of yourself,
the opposite of separation.

Competition
is fighting others
for what you would receive
if you
took the
next step.

The best competition
is always about giving
your own personal best.
The worst competition
is just using another
for not taking the next step.

Your relationship with God
is a reflection
of your relationship
with Yourself

God says to us through others
"If you can love me in this form,
you can go all the way
to Heaven".

Want to be in Heaven
with every person you are with.

You can only attack yourself
in this world;
there is no 'other'.
See the one you are attacking
as your gateway Home.

Seeing God is receiving God.
See everything and all situations
as God,
and have the love take you home.

Everything that has happened
in your life,
Everything you have done,
is a communication.

Compromise
is incomplete communication
Resolution
allows both sides to win.

Do not Compromise
or Adjust
Come to Resolution .

To fill your need
give whatever
you feel
you need.

If you take care of your own needs,
the world will trip over itself
to give you what you want.

If you do not need anything
from another person,
you cannot be
pushed away.

Every need you have
is something which
you defend against receiving.

What you need
you will urgently seek
yet secretly push away.

Everything that is happening
to you, in your world,
can be traced back
to what is happening
in your relationships.

If you don't want to be stuck with how a person or situation is, then You change.

Complaining
  is a combination of
arrogance and powerlessness,
  while believing that
someone else needs to change
  for you.

Complaining is an attack
on your self-image . . . .
you are denying
your personal Power.

Anything
you hold against someone else
you hold against yourself.
All accusations
are Self-accusations.

There are no bad guys
We can all WIN.

What purpose does
   a judgement serve for you?
What don't you have to do ?
What don't you have to receive?

We work hard
for the things
we don't want,
or are afraid to have.

Celebrate
what is given to you.

You and your world
are inextricably tied.
They are one and the same thing.

If you
see a problem,
it's your
problem.

Your experience of your own birth
will create beliefs
that determine how
your children will be born.

If you can heal the experience
of your birth,
you can change
how you have planned
your death.

Revenge
is the heart
of any failure—

The biggest secret
of an independent person
is that
they are still holding on
to someone who broke
their heart.

If it is logically impossible
   for another to get inside of you,
who is the only one
   who could have broken
   your heart ?

The extent to which you control
is the extent
to which you stand in the way of
your success .

We confuse Love
with need.
Love never hurts.
Not getting your needs met
hurts.

You can't feel hurt
unless
you are giving
to take .

When you feel hurt
you are rejecting something
or someone—

All forms of
    blame and grievance
        are merely attempts
    to cover up guilt.

Guilt
    is the great flypaper
        of Life.
We use it
    to hold ourselves back.

Guilt
     is the great withholder.
It is the excuse not to live fully
     for fear of making
          another mistake.
Guilt
     brings about
what you were trying to prevent.
     Ease is freedom from guilt.

When you sow guilt
you reap resentment.

When someone throws guilt at you,
it is a powerful healing method
to accept it · not resist it,
and burn through the feelings
that come up.

It is good to help someone
        not to do something
that will cause them
        to feel guilt.

Not allowing someone
        to abuse you
protects them, as well as you.

When you forgive someone,
you're actually forgiving
the hidden guilt
in yourself.

The only guilt trips
         you accept from others
are the ones you are already
         laying on yourself.

If you feel guilty,
   you will insist on being
   punished in some way;
it feels good temporarily to
   relieve the guilt.
Mistakes
   call only for correction,
      never punishment.

'Shoulds'
   always express
         a Conflict

The more you hold on
the more you push away
that which you could have.

Letting go
is always a way
to move forward.

Letting go
doesn't always give you
what you want,
but it will always give you
what you need.

Letting go
    is a form of giving
that always allows
    for you to receive.

Anytime
    · you are not in wonder
    · transfixed by the beauty
    around you
You are in judgement.

If, through judgement,
you know that you chose—
fear instead of love,
smallness instead of greatness,
just ask:
what am I afraid of knowing
about myself.?

Judgement is always on a person's
personality, body or mistakes.
If you let those things go
there is no problem
in forgiving and joining.

What you give is what you get.
What you take is what you lose.
But either way
you get to choose.

What more could you give
to the people around you
than your own innocence?

We are always in
    the perfect place
to learn the lesson
    we most need to learn.

No one can do anything to you
that you
are not already doing to yourself.

No one can do anything to you
that you are not also doing
at some level .

What you see—
    is what you think you are .
What you experience—
    is what you think you deserve .

The nature of the mind
is Projection.
All thoughts effect
our experience.

If you look at someone
and do not feel love,
all you are seeing
are your own limitations.

The only way
to join with someone
is not to judge them.

Control
is just a way
of covering
fear.

Until you trust someone
you don't love them.

Every experience
is a gift
if rightly seen.

What Life is giving you
is what you are giving
to Life—

If you give,
even though you are feeling pain,
the pain will be healed . . . .
not just for you,
but for those around you as well.

Giving yourself totally
in any situation
creates success.

You expect of others
what you are not willing
to do yourself.

Your purpose leads to your fulfilment, but you may feel unworthy or try to control good feeling so as not to be overwhelmed. These are just symptoms of fear that lead you away from your Truth, your Vision and your Greatness.

To be oneself
is to star in your own Life

Your purpose
    isn't something you do;
It is something
    you are .

Victims
always get to be right
about something...
... sometimes dead right.

In every area you are not succeeding
you are being
right.

Righteousness
is just a compensation
for 'Wrongteousness'.

When you give up the role of
'The Helper',
your ability to help
increases tenfold.

It is only through
            Commitment
that you get to receive.

Your vision is your true direction.
It is a birth of creativity and love.
It is a level of connectedness
with yourself, life and others
that remembers ease.
Most people are afraid of birth,
because if they woke up in the
middle of their birth they would
think they were dying. ∝ But
whatever labor is necessary for
your Vision is a labor of love
that can be both easy · creative ·
and full of love and support.

There are two types of passion:
one comes from the urgency of needs;
the other comes from
the joy of total giving.

To a Perfectionist
anything less than perfection
is failure.

L ove
stops Time—
and starts Eternity.

If you don't feel, you die,
because it is through feeling
that you find meaning
and purpose.

If feeling is shut down
you have to create
excitement and pain
in order to feel alive.

Passion
is taking such a bite out of life
that when the juices
run down your face
everyone licks their lips.

A fight with another
only reflects
a fight within yourself.

Whatever the Conflict
you are only fighting
Yourself.

What you resist
          persists.
You become
that
which you
fight.

We resist only
what we believe
about ourselves.

Ego
is everything
this side of
Oneness.

The masculine part of you gives,
the feminine part of you receives
and in truth they are
inseparable.

If you are to be saved
  it will be through the feminine.

When independent,
        everyone pretends
            to be a man.

The feminine principle is this:
I will take it into me
and transform it.

The extent of your independence
is the extent
to which competition
is ruining your life—

If you don't handle your neurosis,
your neurosis will handle you.

It's not
'seeing is believing'
but
'believing is seeing'.

You cannot see something
in your world
that does not reflect
a part of your own mind.

You blame the other
        when you pull back.
Give yourself so completely
    that you leave yourself
        and become transformed.

To have a miracle
know who you are
and share that knowledge.

To create a miracle
change your mind.

Creating a miracle
is not believing an illusion
through affirming the truth.

Just as when the student is ready
the teacher appears,
when the receiver is ready
the giver appears.

You react to the expectations
you put on yourself
in the same way you react
to the demands others put on you.

When you believe
   you haven't lived up to
someone else's expectations,
in truth
   they haven't lived up to yours.

Whenever you think
someone is using you,
you are actually using them
to hold you back.

Anger
is always a defense
against
a deeper feeling.

You expect
    others to give
what you
    are not giving .

Otherwise
    you would have
no demands or
    hidden agendas .

If something is missing
in your relationship . . . . .
ask yourself
what you
are not giving.

Only when you give
is the door open
for you
to receive.

If there is an area of pain
in your life, have you made it into
a monument to
guilt · revenge
· or righteousness?

Mastery
is the willingness to be innocent
for the sake of
the whole world.

Mastery
is the willingness to be
totally powerful
with integrity.

Mastery
is the irresistible play of God
calling to God.

If you have to prove something
to someone ·
· it means · you don't believe it
yourself .

If you are hurting inside
the quickest way to heal yourself
is to reach out
to someone else in need.

An independent person's
relationship to his body
is akin to that
of a man walking his dog.

The extent of your independence
is proportionate to the extent
that you were wounded
    when you were dependent.

All problems
boil down to one thing:
you have amnesia.
You have forgotten who you are
and what you have come here to do.
Finding your purpose
is one of the greatest healers.

If you put your hope in psychology,
  you are bound for a life of pain.
Put it in creativity · · · ·
    hanging out with your
              Creator.

Without integrity
a man has lost himself.

The extent of your integrity
is the extent to which
you can receive.

No one
can make you feel anything
you don't choose to feel.

Where you
don't feel love in your life
you don't extend yourself,
you feel fear . . . .
and where
you feel fear is where you
get attacked.

The number 1 principle to live by
for the rest of your life:
DO WHAT YOU WANT TO DO!
Doing what you want to do,
with integrity,
is the key to a happy life.

A power struggle
    is a demand on the other
        to meet needs
that could be fulfilled for both
if you just took the next step.

You can only experience fear
if you are trying to live
in the future—

You can only experience guilt
if you are trying to live
in the past

Life will change…
…as you do .

That which has been
done to you
you do to others,
unless you heal
your past.

When attacked,
move towards your attacker,
recognising that the attack was
a call for help. At a deep and
vital level an attacker attacks
you because somewhere they
have a belief that you are the
person who can help them.

It is our fear of giftedness
that complicates life. All problems
have at their root the fear of taking
the next step in life
and the fear of acknowledging ⌒
our gifts and talents.

These so-called problems
are resolved with ease and
simplicity by acknowledging
our life - enhancing gifts
and unwrapping our
Presence.

If someone close to you
loses,
you end up paying
the bill.

Appreciation
moves us out of comparison
and envy.

Asking Heaven's help
makes any job easy.

If you're working hard,
something
is not working.

If you join with someone
who is attacking you,
there would be no resistance,
and therefore
nothing to attack

Happiness
takes no
Prisoners.

This is the acid test for
Trust :
if you have it
you have
no
problem.

All pain
    is the result
        of misunderstanding .

Those around you
are in service to your mind.
God comes at you
in 1,000 disguises
to show you the ways
you keep yourself from Him.

Wherever there is attachment
there is fear.

All pain
   comes from attachment.

Pain___
   is just an unlearned lesson.
It's your mind's way of saying
that you have made a mistake.

You were given practice
for your purpose in life
through the family
in which you grew up.

Your conspiracy is merely this:
What problem did you come to heal
for your family,
and how have you punished yourself
for thinking you failed ?

If your love partner
doesn't reflect your hidden side
your kids will ....
and you can't divorce your kids.

When you are working very hard
in the present,
it means you haven't let go
of the past.

If you waste time,
time wastes you.

Much has been said about giving,
but giving without receiving
is merely sacrifice · · · · · ·
· Someone is called upon to lose
for others to win.

Abundance is the recognition
of our innocence,
and our ability to receive.

What you have in your life
    reflects what you really want,
rather than
    what you think you want.

How much you have of
anything
is exactly how much of it
you think you deserve .

Not receiving
is an act
of Revenge.

When you can give yourself
totally to another person,
you can begin to see
who they are.

What you hold against someone
  who didn't care for you in the past,
holds you up now...
  from being loved in the present.

What we haven't forgiven
our parents for,
we do
to others.

Your parents birthed you
and did what they could for you..
then you made them your scapegoat
and you've been pinning
                your problems
        on them ever since .

We left Heaven
because we thought
we had a better answer
than God's.

We are all doing
the best we can
given inner
and
outer circumstances.

Whatever lessons you haven't learned
with your mother / father,
you will attempt to learn
with your daughter / son.

Heaven
    can only be natural now,
    never in an instant replay.

Vision . . .
is giving Everything
while holding on to Nothing.

The essence of sex
        is communication.
All the rest is just
        the plumbing.

Sex is basically a form of communication that reflects the flow of our relationship to life. As such it becomes a catch-all for any unresolved or unfinished business.

To let sex always be a love-making is to know the true meaning of communication.

The unfinished business of
relationships of the past
will show itself in
relationships of the present.

Every goodbye
that is complete
creates a new beginning.

You can blame another
only
at the cost of your own
freedom .

If you don't have
something you want in your life
ask yourself :
· with whom are you in
a power struggle?
· on whom are you getting revenge?
· of what are you afraid?
If you don't have something,
it is because you have been
in control .

Grievances come from
the unmet demand
that people do things
your way.

Roles and duties
    are built on grievances
and the feeling that you are
    a failure.
You act out a role in an attempt
    to compensate for the failure.
When playing a role
    you look like a success
but – feel like a failure.

Most of us hold on to
what was good in the past
and prevent ourselves
from having it NOW.

Letting go is simply
keeping things
in present perspective.

Not to let go
is to enslave the universe
to your plan for Happiness.
How well has your plan
worked so far
anyway?

Letting go
is the dependent person's way
of saving their relationship
and bringing it
to the next level
of partnership.

Surrender
 is letting go,
  trusting
   and commitment

The birth
you are afraid to take
becomes
your death.

Without competition
   there can't be sacrifice.
Sacrifice is a subtle way
   to feel better than others.

If you truly realized
that you were a child of God,
how could you not but
be in Heaven?
And as you enjoy this,
how could you not but
share the joy?

You don't have to do anything
for God;
but remember Heaven
for everyone.

If God is in all things,
why would he choose
not to be in You?

Life is about
    s-t-r-e-t-c-h-i-n-g—,
not Stretchmarks.

When you are frightened
    of taking the next step
you invite in
    a temptation or a problem
to distract you
    from getting on with your life.

Your happiness
is the best gift
you can give the world.

If you don't accept
where you are,
how can you expect
to move ahead?

No one makes you sacrifice
but yourself.
It comes out of your need for approval
and fear of taking the next step.

To reach enlightenment,
desire nothing,
resist nothing,
but receive everything.

Who do you feel needs
to give you permission
before you can move ahead
in your life— ?
When are you going to start
to give yourself permission?

Vision
is leaping the abyss
to love,
and leaving a bridge
for others to follow.

To intellectualize
is to choose the route
of repression.

Choices made continuously
in the same direction
become an attitude.
Where are you going?

Charisma
is influence
with integrity.

To share your feelings,
not using them
as a weapon or form of blackmail,
and reach the deepest roots
of your awareness,
creates breakthrough.

The areas in which
you don't trust others
are really the areas
in which you don't trust
yourself.

What is not let go of
in the past
        hides the present
as it longs for the future .

A problem
cannot withstand
intimacy .

Sacrifice—
   is not giving.
Sacrifice—
   is counterfeit giving.

Winning does not come
from having losers . . .
that's not true abundance

Wisdom
comes from learning the lesson
that stops the suffering .

In the eleventh hour,
it's either emergence
or emergency.

The secret of Happiness
is to cease to cherish
opinions .

If you really want it,
there is a way!

Whatever abundance
you allow for yourself,
you give permission
for others to receive .

Indulgence
    is a form of avoidance,
You need to rest up from it
as much as you do
        from sacrifice.
    Indulgence doesn't satisfy,
because it doesn't allow you
        to receive.

The greatest fear
is the fear
of Happiness.

The greatest art is to be oneself. This naturally proceeds from living your purpose · rather than living for approval . Otherwise you could end up in the obituaries under someone else's name. Your purpose is what you , of all people in the world, can do best. Most people are frightened of their own purpose, and are thus frightened of their own Love Passion and Happiness .

There are moments that we spend
in the source of life .
From each of us burns a light,
a candle of hope
Without even one of us
the darkness breeds.
We are each of us, a mirror of life.
The beauty is so quick
So full of feeling
that to be touched by it
is never again to say
'I am not you'
When this is so, life never ceases
to be an event
of Wonder.